The days of spring

Dhanya Gupta

BookLeaf
Publishing

Presentation by *BookLeaf Publishing*

Web: www.bookleafpub.com

E-mail: info@bookleafpub.com

ISBN: 978-93-5769-301-1

First edition 2022

Table of Contents

~The days of spring~

All miles away
Keep that love alive;

The day I picked up the pen...

**Not only had I picked up the pen,
But also I looked out of the window.
And realized I was philophobic,
And managing myself to stay away from toxics;
Fear of mine is so intense that find it,
Near my softest pillow where I find
My feeling overflowing….**

Penning down my thoughts
Has been a long way of mine to express;
Time is running away, along with moments made
Have been crashing down my world's mess…

Writing about days,
Where everything pictures perfect, huh?
Writing about days,
Where everything seemed perfect;
I've felt shattered while time held me close,
Held closely by melancholy wrapped in its arms;

Writing is a waste of time,
Who says?
I guess you haven't tried yet!
Trust me,

Nothing is better than this
Keeping your diary near
Instead of wrapped in melancholy's charm…..

This comfort and relaxation, I get,
Acquired when I pour it out on my paper;
Been philophobic and disengaged from the
World,
Not saying this
Just penning down my thoughts,
Stuck out in my head….

And here, keeping my pen down for a second
I got something
My diary ☺

My diary- my 'best friend'

It went like,
A thousand memories
A thousand inside jokes
A thousand secrets, deep secrets….
And with only one reason to tell;
A best friend…

Strengthening my interest
Towards my diary
Had made me a better person than before
Whenever I flip the pages
Of my memories; of my diary
It takes me to the moment spent restored;

The speaking word with double commas
Take me somewhere out of this world,
The careless words used
Made me wept in torrents,
And I understood
I was the happiest version of mine then,
Peaceful, and in a calm stage
Because maybe I had this once….

Diary has been a chronicle of all my past buried
hatchets
It's been a drug to me; I can read it over and over
The smell of diary is still aromatic, even without any
scent
Because it holds 'you' and my memories together…

You have been a path to all my problems,
Always beside me
You and I both have gone through much in life,
But writing to you is my treasured choice…

A day without my best friend seems irritable
For me to deal,
That's the main reason, why I always feel complete~!
I have discovered my best friend inside the pages of my
diary
And I wish all the best to you too… :)

A 'whole bunch of love'

She's lying you can tell me from a mile away,
She notices each and everything but acts as never
discerned.
She knew well, that one day, he'll go miles away,
And she even knew, she'll be all alone, keeping that
love alive

Looking forward to those blossoms of life,
Those moments,
Those miles,
Those pacifications of her life,
Are buried inside my mind;

Bringing peace to place and peace to war
On a horrendous day
She never came into prominence as a woman.
Struggling with those terrific moments,
 With love and fear.

What if, she would break someone's heart?
And the person does the same!

What if, she would fall in love with someone?
And the person does the same!

What if, she knew he was wrong?
And the person knows the same!

What if, she betrays someone's trust?
And the person does the same!

People do often judge,
On these agitated days, she still looks upon who she is!
People do begin to blather,
On these frantic days, she still knows who she needs!

She's sanguine about prospects of life,
She's even more certain about life,
She knows, how to bind everything even on awful days,
Because she knew how to love and express.
She knows, how to mend broken relationships,
Because she knows how to deal and struggle….

Don't you carry her bunch of love?

The Essence of life...

**In the essence of life, she tried to conceal every
sorrow and pain,
In the essence of life, she knows that it's challenging
but without caring, she continues for herself
To be herself,
In the essence of life,
A woman is an embodiment of beauty, intelligence,
veracity
And uprightness.**

It comes within her personification;
Her spirit lightens up her world and whatever she
performs.
She's an inspiration for all of us out there,
She's there to tell us the beauty of a woman.
She's much more than just the beauty of her face and
body.

Her spirit, her sense of self-worth, her decision-making
power,
Her access to opportunities and resources, and her
belief of believing in herself is as much strengthened as
Himalayas.

Her ability to change the nature, her ability to conceal everything inside her,
The essence of the life of a woman is the beauty lying within her.

She is a woman, not an oddball,
She always hangs in there to prove herself.
And that initial phase passes as time flies,
It requires a lot of effort, time, sacrifices, adjustments, and patience.

She keeps herself to be a part of old reminiscent memories.
The mindset of the people keeps her away from all her desires,
But she believes that she has to deal with them.

She's a bit weird but crazy,
She's a bit passionate but flawless.
Her mistakes are mistaken due to her passion for aggressiveness,
She needs you for her silly demands and her worth for stubbornness.
Her imperfections are too much for you, to undergo.
But her keenness to love without fear and any condition just drove her away out of fear.

She never wanted to be the reason for herself to
abandon all her dreams,
She chose her happiness over her dreams for herself.
Because she's a phantom of charm,
She continues with dealing and suffering from horrific
hallucinations.
She's just like a blooming flower,
Needs time, but when it blooms it's enough to beautify
the whole garden.
 Even roses with thorns appear endurable.

She's an exquisite woman,
For so long, I believed that it was hard to understand,
but now I came to know.
That associating being with her who is hard to love, but
being lost,
I misunderstood that she is diminishing her love for
everyone.
Because now she lives for herself because she believes,
That she's her priority herself.

You!!

Sometimes,
Some feelings
Are there to pursue escape
But that doesn't mean, I am not with YOU.

It's ok if you are not there,
It's ok if you feel everything is fine, it is!!
We both are going through some or the other phase,
And it's ok if you find it right.
It's just a matter of time, it will be fine and we'll be
together again.

A little more every day treats every time an every you
new,
At my own pace!
A pace towards destiny has chosen you for me,
And I am following it, trust me.
Just be ready and steady towards something
approaching,
Towards you, love.
That I am near you, staying within you…

It's nothing indeed that you are going through
But the matter of time is growing though inside us!
Let your happy tears be there or sad smiles

Or whatever you have on your face, let it escape.
Because I am with you and will be WITH YOU…
We both are going through some or the other phase,
And it's ok if you find it right.

Binding together, those broken threads

If she ever falls in love,
Promise her, you won't declare in the whole world.
Because she loves you, not the world,
Keep it within you.

The world is always standing beside to ruin and destroy everything,
Even the beautiful things built,
Keep it to your own 'top-secret'.

If she ever falls in love,
She knows how to retain promises.
She says 'hearts and promises are the most fragile essence of life',
It's just like they are made of glass,
If you do not take care, they will break and shatter into pieces,
In the end, subsequently, they can be fixed, but will not be the same.
You will break it, into crumbles.
But it's ok; she knows how to mend…..

If she ever falls in love,
Do not get scared.
She is there for you,
She knows love is a wall of promises and trust,
But she wants you not to get scared to fear falling,
She will be clasping it.

If she ever falls in love….

I found shelter in every storm

Some bonds,
Are a way to beautify them
And hustling to name them
Are left unnamed...

Some feelings
Are so beautiful;
That they are left unsaid.

Ruining your beautiful moments,

Tieing them within a boundary of assumptions.
Let them be as fiercest, as they could in a storm,
Some or the day, it will slow down
Just wait for the moment.

Let them be free, and welcome them in your home,
Where YOU find your peace and shelter in this
ferocious storm…
Above ahead, where the storm wilds
There is a tree that may be broken or damaged,

I want you to slow down and sit under its shed.
And we get to receive how it all began between us..!

A world of issues,
Invisible lying there near you
But felt to the deepest of the beat of yours
And the course of every drop of blood
Flowing through it!
A wild storm of ME and You, wilding there
Tangling with the broken branch,
Like a delicate broken heart :)

All I have a dream is to fulfill-

Dear ahead,
I want you to wait for me
Because we are together on this path
If you move ahead, I will be all alone
Except for my unfulfilled dream

Breaking all those negative walls of expectations,
And looking towards the positive fulfillments of my
dream
I received a dream with positiveness….
People are seen seeking love, is one getting it?
What is love without an unfulfilled dream?
No one has answers,
To this;
It's just an empty decorated box.

While struggling with such
People will make you responsible for the lack
Needed,
Instead of choosing to elevate it
Higher,
The thing about all life is to go with the flow
Regardless of who comes with you:)
And fulfills the lack needed.

Your dream can be accomplished,
If you work on it;
A dream of mine is fulfilled;
Admitting this…

Your dream deserves it's fulfilled one back,
Your love wants to love again,
You need your dream to love you again.
Your time needs your mind and heart to respond,
Your belief needs your support to look upon,
And you need to keep your dream alive again…

A shine of support ☺

Those tales narrated by you, dear diary
And maybe you'll ask me why?
Just because we were together sharing successes,
failures and even stupidly funny anecdotes talked
about…
There was never even a flicker of judgment,
Always was a shine of support, acceptance, and love.
That's the main secret to remembering all this!

A day when becomes night...

The blur of the sky faded away gradually
And it was a bright morning again
With a new hope and bright sun
And a day became night in a snap~

I always embrace the sunrise carrying its breathtaking
sunshine
With appreciation for a new day welcoming.
The sun slowly lets down,
Maybe a bit faster than before now and then…

I observe it with the greatest admiration
As fast as could sky turns black,
To welcome night with its bright city lights
The sky was aflame with the fire of the twilight.

The whitish demilune moon shone fulgently like a
diamond
Dazzling in the sky,
I have being a selenophile; falling in love with moon
I looked up at the starry night that extended infinitely…
The days are beautiful because we can pursue and bring
out our dreams,
Nights are even more alluring because we get time to
see new dreams to bring out.

Lying on a hot Sunday night
I buried myself under a blanket,
That warmed my legs and slowly,
I found myself drenched in sweat and tension
Just then, I embraced the night,
And went to sleep tight;

The first time, I saw you in the ocean...

Everything happened for the first and the last time...

The first time I saw you near the ocean sitting beside me,
Keeping your hands above mine, holding them tightly.
I can conquer my innermost demons to let them swim in the deepest ocean near me,
I wish I could tell you where once lay an emptiness, I never knew you too existed
To fill up my existence...

The waves became higher and stronger,
You wanted me to write this down near my pages.
You wanted to pull me to the shoreline,
The fierce waves were just endless;
I was able to hear every heartbeat of mine
It went as if waves were coming near me and leaving me in a snap...

And just then, you left me:
I watched you in anguish, you fading away from me
slowly and gradually
I wanted to stop you, but I couldn't…

My heart was in my mouth,
Was filled with fear because I understood you were not
there to die.
For a moment, I convinced myself, I was left with
nothing to do,
And you disappeared.
You have made me a thalassophobic just then….

The pages of your heart began to weep taking me
along,
I won't be able to tell you about my life adventures
anymore,
 "We are separated".
I bid goodbye to you, which I wanted never to do,
But I'm happy; at least you carry what we made
together,
Our together- moments, our memories, me and you…

I know, you know better than me that time heals
everything,
But those open written pages describe everything….
<About me and you, my DEAR diary>>>>>

The dawn of the day

**In the month of spring, the first dawn of the day,
Brought a smile to my face.
I perceived something fixed and full of pure joy,
And I realized that I got you back.
It was just a nightmare, but all nightmares do not
come true,
Unless it's mine!**

The proverb as states,
'Bluebirds are a sign of spring; warm weather and
gentle south breezes they bring'
A chorus of bird's song goes along,
Spring brings happiness, motivation, and positivity.
Among all of us,
A feeling of aspiration brings beauty to our life.

When the month of spring arrives,
Everything seems pretty and adorable;
Don't you think?
The sun's first sunshine,
The chirping of birds
States your morning as a perfect day;

The person you see as soon as you wake up,
Won't you believe it?
The buzzing of trees goes along
Taking the beauty of nature together!

Sirens in the distance...

Still, till today those siren sounds haunt me,
And every time a siren sounds, I wonder if you are
around.
But you aren't there,
Cuz you know this better, I'd do it all again!
A thousand miles between us now,
It causes me to wonder how our love tonight
remained so strong.
It makes our risk tight all along,
Still, till today, those siren sounds haunt me.

Your sirens always, every time make me feel
You are there somewhere,
I don't know why is this so..
But as far as I know, since you left, everything is just
not fine to deal with!

I'm not saying to come back,
Because that's not possible;
All I want you to always be there whenever I need you,
Is that possible?

I wished I could stop that moment
I didn't want to cry, I tried to be staying tough,

But still, I couldn't stand looking at your dispassionate
face.
Cherishing every moment there,
All I was left to do!

The unknown, in words!!

Things are unknown,
But you are unrevealed.

The day I met you, you seem mysterious to me
I wanted to get intrigued by you,
By telling you each and everything
And by knowing your unknown stories;

When I found you, you were nameless,
You remained undisclosed.
But since I got you, I got myself!

And when I lost you,
I tried hard to reach you, but I can't hide.
How strong I was once I was with you,
But now, things have changed taking me along by my
side…

I know, you too miss my presence,
But I've not got one like you.
Since you left……

Those stories which I knew once,
Appears unknown, in words!!!

Someone's there, to tell me spring has come...

Oh, you're there! You two naughty ones!
Spring has come! The time of flowers and plants
brings a new life to them…

I saw you, my little plant
Sitting near me,
Appreciating the raindrops,
You and I found peace there…

My little plant
I know, YOU have gone through so much
For your growth,
Now the rain is learning you well.

Last night, I saw you there
Rustling with the leaves
It's difficult to cope with life
But now it grieves…
Spring is already here
On trees, leaves are getting green,
Flowers are blooming on the deserted land
In your heart,

Trust me, we are happy
With tears ;)

A season of love,
The natural world resuscitates and reinvigorates.
And I am glued with the memories, written in you…

Does time heals everything?

Getting hurt by the time,
But make sure you take time out
To heal yourself

Time grows and heals eventually, sometimes it takes
Days, months, or even years fathom its extremity...
In an era of fairy tales are exquisitely depicted,
Offering us false hopes and a provisional refuge
From the truths of life,
Time hurts and heals everything.

How arduous is to let memories slip,
And not get a chance to confess about
All the butterflies you feel.

The time when I got lost in some moment, the urge to
Stop that time for long,
The reality is to open and live my heart at a point and
let it
Feel the touch of a broken spot of my heart to revive to
Stay happy again!

Time is there, it will heal
Why to be tensed?
Time is there, it will heal

Why to feel sad?
Time is there, it will heal
It heals everything, as time passes by.

With over-involvement, ups, and downs in life
All I want to do is to steal all moments of love and
Happiness
And save them into the pockets of my heart
To use them when I feel low or time does not
respond…

Does it??
…
It does!!
…

To the one, I always want to see smiling<3

Hey you there,
Everything you have gone through, we
understand…
Why not give your life a second chance,
What say?

I know, things get mischievous some times
But you need to make them placate,
I know, it feels like the leaves feel in autumn!
But you need to relish in the rain!

You need to whirl-twirl in the moonlight
You need to laugh madly on even the lamest jokes
And you need to terminate your pain out.

Better days are yet to come,
Make you the happiest version of yours
Have faith in your life,
Something is yet to be yours…

The pain; the agony you are facing is going to make
you
Even more well-built

At any moment, you feel things are not appropriate
Just give a minute to your growth,
It will cherish you and your well-built memories
Never going to fade away;

The things you have attained are enough to hurt you
But I want you to be your strongest version; ever been
before
Seeing you in the moonlight,
Was as if the highlight of my day!

A life half *lived & lied*

**A life half lived
A life half lied**

**A life just lived by lying
A life just lying and lived**

We are standing under a shade of a tree,
But still I can feel raindrops falling on my heart
Things are being as they want to be
Living a life, which maybe I never wanted; though my
heart

 I can feel the moon when it smiles at me
Makes me believe a new day; a new morning tomorrow
A life just going through something not acceptable
A life just living with lies in a row…

Not just concluding an epilogue

Just penning down my thoughts,
What about you?

. . . .

www.ingramcontent.com/pod-product-compliance
Lightning Source LLC
La Vergne TN
LVHW041246200726
843507LV00013B/2831